DARWINISM

TODAY

THE TRUTH ABOUT CINDERELLA

A DARWINIAN VIEW OF PARENTAL LOVE

Martin Daly and Margo Wilson

Yale University Press
New Haven and London

Published 1998 in Great Britain by Weidenfeld & Nicolson.
Published in the United States 1999 by Yale University Press.
Copyright © 1998 by Martin Daly and Margo Wilson.
Foreword copyright © 1998 by Helena Cronin and Oliver Curry.

Printed in the United States of America.

Library of Congress Cataloging-in-Publication Data:

Daly, Martin, 1944–
     The truth about Cinderella : a Darwinian view of parental love
/ Martin Daly and Margo Wilson.
          p.   cm. — (Darwinism today)
     Includes bibliographical references.
     ISBN 0-300-08029-8 (cloth : alk. paper)
     1. Stepparents. 2. Parent and child. 3. Child abuse.
4. Stepfamilies—Folklore. I. Wilson, Margo. II. Title. III. Series.
HQ759.92.D35   1999
306.874—dc21   99-28271
                              CIP

A catalogue record for this book is available from the British Library.

The paper in this book meets the guidelines for permanence and
durability of the Committee on Production Guidelines for Book
Longevity of the Council on Library Resources.

10   9   8   7   6   5   4   3   2   1

CONTENTS

....

The Series Editors thank
Peter Tallack for his help

FOREWORD

Darwinism Today is a series of short books by leading figures in the field of evolutionary theory. Each title is an authoritative pocket introduction to the Darwinian ideas that are setting today's intellectual agenda.

The series developed out of the Darwin@LSE programme at the London School of Economics. The Darwin Seminars provide a platform for distinguished evolutionists to present the latest Darwinian thinking and to explore its application to humans. The programme is having an enormous impact, both in helping to popularize evolutionary theory and in fostering cross-disciplinary approaches to shared problems.

With the publication of **Darwinism Today** we hope that the best of the new Darwinian ideas will reach an even wider audience.

Helena Cronin and Oliver Curry
Series Editors

DARWIN@ 🔲

THE
TRUTH ABOUT
CINDERELLA

··

A DARWINIAN VIEW OF
PARENTAL LOVE

CHAPTER 1

··

Folk Tales

Around the World with Cinderella

The abused stepchild is one of the stock characters of folklore. Cinderella, of which there are hundreds of variants, is probably the best-known example. In the usual version, the poor girl's mother has died and her father has remarried a dreadful woman, who brings two daughters from a prior marriage to her new home. With Cinderella's wicked stepmother reigning in the domestic sphere, the girls are treated far from equitably. The heroine is unjustly relegated to the status of household slave, while her father is chronically off stage and apparently oblivious to her degradation. However, virtue eventually prevails, with a bit of supernatural assistance, and Cindy marries a prince. We needn't belabour the details, since almost everyone knows the story.

'Stop right there,' interjects an imagined reader. 'Maybe everyone in our culture knows the story, but Westerners are not "almost everyone".'

That's true, ours is just one of many cultural traditions. But we were not being ethnocentric. It really is true that virtually everyone, everywhere, is familiar with stories about unjustly mistreated stepchildren. Of course, the stories aren't all identical right down to the pumpkins and the glass slippers. Anyone who has read the Grimm Brothers' fairy tales already knows that, since these pioneer folklorists collected a diversity of cruel stepmother stories from European sources, including *Cinderella* and *Snow White* and *Hansel and Gretel* and *The Juniper Tree*. But there is nothing special about European tradition in this regard. Innocent children are victimized by vicious, neglectful, exploitative stepmothers and stepfathers in folklore all over the world. Cinderella's cruel domestic situation is iconic.

According to an old Japanese story, quite like *Cinderella* but apparently of independent origin, 'Benizara was a very honest and gentle girl, but her stepmother was very cruel to her.' This heroine's decency gains her solace and assistance from both friends and strangers, and she eventually wins the heart of a nobleman by extemporizing a more beautiful poem than her stepsister Kakezara is able to do. The wicked stepmother makes a final desperate attempt to substitute Kakezara deceitfully for Benizara, but accidentally kills her own daughter in the process.

Other stories have happy endings that don't involve besting a stepsister or marrying a prince. A nineteenth-century translation of the Russian *Baba Yaga* begins 'Once upon a time there was an old couple. The husband lost his wife and married again. But he had a daughter by the first marriage, a young girl, and she found no favour in the eyes of her evil stepmother, who used to beat her, and consider how she could get her killed outright.' This fairy tale's stepmother has an even more horrible sister, a cannibalistic witch into whose clutches the stepmother tries to send the innocent girl, saying, 'Go to your aunt, my sister.' But the heroine consults her '*real* aunt' first and learns how to escape the witch. The story ends: 'As soon as her father heard all about it, he became wroth with his wife, and shot her. But he and his daughter lived on and flourished, and everything went well with them.'

Things don't always end well for the abused child. The Naga people of northern India say that the monkeys that steal their crops are the descendants of Murimong and Thanian, two children who found this debased way of life preferable to staying with a stepmother who fed them rotten food. Elsewhere, the stepmothers of folklore butcher the children and serve them up to their gormless husbands, or falsely accuse their stepsons of sexual assault and thereby dupe the boys' fathers into banishing or killing them.

And what about stepfathers? Folk wisdom has it that

3

they, too, are a menace. According to a sixteenth-century French proverb with many parallels elsewhere:

> *Quand la femme se remarie ayant enfants,*
> *Elle leur fait un ennemi pour parent.*
>
> (The mother of babes who elects to rewed
> Has taken their enemy into her bed.)

Fairy tales about malevolent stepfathers are scarcer than those about stepmothers, but no cheerier. The great American encyclopaedist of folklore, Stith Thompson, recognized just two 'motifs' for stepfathers: 'cruel' and 'lustful'.

These maxims and tales cannot be arbitrary or chance inventions. The characters and their conflicts are too consistent. When the stories are of exotic origin, the protagonists' occupations and even to some extent their aspirations may seem strange, but step-parental antipathy is one dependable element. With a little effort one can find an occasional story like the Icelandic *Tale of Hildur, the Good Stepmother*, but such a story is the exception that proves the rule: its very title implies a celebration of exceptional, out-of-character virtue, and is predicated on the wickedness of the stock villainesses of what Icelanders call *stjupmaedrasagas*.

Stereotypical step-parents

Scholars have debated whether the uncannily similar Cinderella stories of Asia, Europe, and elsewhere represent numerous separate inventions or the spread of one or a few ur-stories instead. But in a sense it doesn't matter. The cross-cultural ubiquity of Cinderella stories is revealing in either case, for they would not persist where their themes had no resonance. Those themes must have something to do with the human condition.

Psychoanalytically oriented folklorists have proposed that cruel stepmothers are symbolic representations of the hostile or uncaring side of natural mothers, and that this splitting helps the child deal with maternal inconsistency and its own ambivalence. But even if this be so, why should people everywhere choose a stepmother to fill this particular symbolic role? The unstated premise would seem to be that she has a prior, archetypal identity as hostile and uncaring. And step-relationship is, indeed, a dominant metaphor for lack of care. The *Oxford English Dictionary*, for example, defines 'stepmotherly' as 'harsh or neglectful', and there are numerous parallels in other languages. The official Japanese botanical name of the wickedly spiney broad-leaved plant *Polygonum senticosum* is Mamako-no-shiri-nugui: the stepchild's bottom-wiper.

Is it truly the case that step-parents are relatively exploitative, neglectful, and cruel? Ordinary people think so. Several studies of perceptions and expectations of step-relationships have recently been conducted, mainly in the United States, and the results consistently indicate that such relationships are viewed at least somewhat pessimistically and pejoratively. People expect imaginary characters identified as step-parents to be more distant and less supportive of the children than otherwise identical characters identified as the 'natural' parents, a presumption of difference that is reduced but not eliminated among raters who have actually lived in stepfamilies. But of course ordinary people also believe in horoscopes and saintly interventions and the immortality of Elvis, so the prevalence of these convictions can hardly be considered evidence for their validity.

In other words, step-parental wickedness *might* be just a popular fiction in spite of it all, and this is a possibility that clearly appeals to many writers. Those social scientists who have demonstrated negative perceptions of step-relationships usually refer to them as *stereotypes* and *myths*, rather than using more neutral descriptive terms such as *beliefs* or *expectations* or *generalizations*. Moreover, insofar as stepfamily life really does entail difficulties, researchers in this area have not hesitated to contend that the stereotypes and myths *cause* the problems.

But before we start arguing about the determinants of stepfamily 'dysfunction', it would be nice to have some notion of what we're trying to explain. What are the simple epidemiological facts about problems in one family circumstance versus another? Do children really incur risks of various sorts when one parent dies or departs and the remaining parent takes a new partner? And if so, to what degree: are we talking about a slight elevation of risk, or something more dramatic? These would seem to be rather obvious questions for research, but as we shall see, they have been surprisingly neglected. And that is unfortunate, because it turns out that the risk differentials are immense.

Children who reside with one (presumed) genetic parent — the term we prefer to 'natural' or 'biological' parent, since there is nothing unnatural about substitute parenthood — and one step-parent — the term we shall use to refer to one who lives with an opposite-sex partner and is thereby *in loco parentis* to the partner's resident child or children of prior unions, regardless of marital registration — incur massive increases in the rates of the most severe forms of child maltreatment. Having a step-parent has turned out to be the most powerful epidemiological risk factor for severe child maltreatment yet discovered.

CHAPTER 2

....

Behaving Like Animals

Infanticidal coups

There is another, quite different, line of thought by which one could arrive at the hypothesis that step-parents will tend to nurture children less solicitously than genetic parents and will be more likely to misuse them. Contemporary theory and research concerning animal social behaviour provide a rationale for expecting parents to be discriminative in their care and affection, and more specifically, to discriminate in favour of their own young. These expectations derive from consideration of how evolution works, and since the human animal has evolved by the same Darwinian processes as other animals, there is no apparent reason why the same principles should not apply.

Consider, for example, the social behaviour of the African lion, the 'king of beasts'. A lion pride is a social group that hunts and defends a territory co-operatively. The pride is matrilineal: a typical female grows up and eventually breeds in the group into which she was born, whereas males disperse at maturity. One result is that the adult females in the pride are almost always close kin: sisters and cousins, mothers and daughters, aunts and nieces. The two or three or four adult males associated with the pride were born elsewhere, perhaps dispersing from a common natal pride together, perhaps teaming up as roving bachelors. They attained their current status by displacing another coalition of males, probably a coalition diminished in numbers or formidability by age, and the new coalition's reign will last only a few years, at best, before they too are displaced.

After a pregnancy of about 110 days, a lioness nurses her cubs for about eighteen months. The hormonal state induced by this nursing inhibits ovulation and hence delays the mother's next pregnancy, as it does in other mammals including *Homo sapiens*. The result is that almost two years will pass between one litter's birth and the next if the first litter survives until weaning. However, if some mishap befalls the cubs, then their mother's milk will dry up and her next pregnancy will occur sooner.

Thus, when a coalition of young males succeeds in taking over a pride, one or more of the resident females is apt to be nursing dependent young, and it may be many months before such nursing females will be ready to mate again. So how do the new males respond to the cubs sired by their predecessors? The grisly answer is that they systematically search them out and kill them.

Killing a deposed predecessor's young is now known to occur in a wide variety of vertebrate and invertebrate animals. The perpetrators are usually males, but not always. Among the tropical marsh-dwelling birds called jaçanas, for example, familiar sex roles are reversed. A large territorial female may have as many as four smaller males occupying subterritories within hers. Each male builds his own nest and incubates four of her eggs in it, and he then guards the precociously mobile young without female assistance. But if one female jaçana displaces a rival and thereby acquires a little harem of dutiful fathers, she conscientiously goes about breaking the eggs of her predecessor.

As horrifying as such behaviour may appear to the human observer, it is clearly not pathological. Indeed, its rationale is so compelling that the interesting questions are why it was not investigated and understood sooner, and why it is not even more widely distributed in the animal kingdom than it is. A mate's parental efforts may be considered a sort of 'resource', and it should be no surprise to a Darwinian that when male lions or female jaçanas gain control of that resource, they make sure that it is spent promoting their own reproductive success rather than that of their rivals.

Natural selection as reproductive competition

Until about thirty years ago, many biological scientists subscribed to an unexamined 'greater goodism' (in philosopher Helena Cronin's felicitous phrase), interpreting the behaviour of animals as means to the end of 'reproducing the species'. This interpretation was wrong. Darwinian selection, the process that gave form to animals and all their complex functional parts, does not in general produce creatures with attributes tailored to promote species goals. How could it? Selection is overwhelmingly a matter of the differential survival and reproduction of variants within a species.

In any sexually reproducing population, females are engaged in a sort of 'zero-sum game' — a contest in which one's gain is necessarily another's loss — over shares of the maternity of the next generation. The males are simultaneously engaged in a parallel contest over shares of paternity. The result is that selection favours those traits and genes that have whatever it takes to out-reproduce the alternative traits and genes of one's same-sex, same-species rivals.

Of course some of the traits that evolve as a result of this competitive process may contribute to the species' survival and proliferation. Anti-predator adaptations like fleetness and keen senses are likely examples. But other selectively favoured traits certainly do not promote the greater good. The stag's spectacular antlers, for example, are energetically expensive and probably make him (and his hinds) more conspicuous to predators as well. Collectively, a League of Stag Brethren would be better off if there were no such structures. Unfortunately there isn't any League of Stag Brethren. There are simply individual stags, bumping heads with one another for breeding rights.

Why should we not expect acting on behalf of a collective like a lion pride to evolve by natural selection? Well, suppose there were a mutant variety of lion who refrained from killing his predecessors' offspring and simply waited until the lioness was ready to breed again. The duration of that wait would presumably reflect an interbirth interval that had evolved to best promote the female's own reproductive posterity – leaving aside the complication that it could represent a compromise between the lioness's optimal interbirth interval and that favoured by her cubs – and such a wait might very well maximize the reproductive success of the pride or even the species. But how would the infanticidal mutant fare in reproductive competition with males who ensured that females under their control were not wasting time and milk replicating some other males' genes? The simple fact that the mutant would on average have to wait longer for a female in his pride to conceive his young guarantees that the infanticidal form will win the reproductive competition, if other things are equal, and the prosocial mutant form will go extinct.

This sort of reasoning is implicit in the logic of natural selection. Nevertheless, fully a hundred years after Darwin (1809–82) and Wallace (1823–1913) announced their (mutually independent) discovery of natural selection at an 1858 meeting of the Linnaean Society, few biologists really seemed to get it. Both popular and professional works routinely claimed that animals give their lives so that others can live and reproduce; populations were uncritically presumed to regulate their size in order to avoid depleting their resource bases; and even such spectacles as stags fighting over hinds were interpreted by the Nobel Prize winner Konrad Lorenz as public-spirited games played for the purpose of arriving at a consensual identification of the best breeding stock. These greater-goodist accounts of animal social and reproductive behaviour were prevalent not because their proponents rejected orthodox Darwinism, but because their logical inconsistency with orthodox Darwinism went unnoticed.

A Darwinian revolution in ethology

This situation began to improve in the 1960s, thanks to the efforts of several clear thinkers. Using ingenious field research and data analysis, Oxford ornithologist David Lack (1910–73) demonstrated that birds and mammals do not refrain from excessive reproduction in order to avoid population explosions, as greater-goodists had supposed, but in fact produce as many viable young as they can. Meanwhile, a young theoretical biologist named William Hamilton was exploring the implications of the fact that an individual's success in replicating her genes is a function not only of personal reproduction but also of her effects on the survival and reproduction of non-descendant relatives. Using this broadened conception of 'inclusive fitness' effects, Hamilton showed how even the most selfless and apparently public-spirited animal behaviour, such as the labours of sterile worker bees, could be explained as products of ordinary Darwinian selection. Finally, in 1966, George Williams published his masterly *Adaptation and Natural Selection: A Critique of Some Current Evolutionary Thought* in which he demolished a number of prominent greater-goodist just-so stories. These developments laid the groundwork for more sophisticated Darwinian thinking: the selectionist, adaptationist theories and research of modern behavioural ecology and sociobiology.

The ensuing years were heady times for animal behaviourists. Game theory was applied to the problem of explaining how aggressive contests unfold. Courtship displays, hitherto interpreted merely as ways of indicating one's species and communicating one's physiological preparedness to breed, were newly elucidated as propaganda, aimed at sceptical potential mates whose interests differ from those of the displayer. Parental care of the young came to be seen as a contested arena, in which each offspring seeks more of the parent's limited resources than would be optimal from the parental perspective. Certain aspects of social behaviour, such as to what extent mates are faithful in a given species or to what extent fathers help raise the young, came to be seen as the resolution of conflicts between individuals with different agendas, such as same-sex rivals and potential mates. Hence they were compromises that might be ideal for no one. Fieldworkers had a host of new ideas to test, and most of the things that we thought we understood seemed to need re-examination.

As recently as 1966, Konrad Lorenz (1903–89) had authoritatively asserted that 'the aim of aggression is never lethal'. With the new emphasis on selection, this claim was soon challenged. One such challenge was primatologist Sarah Hrdy's carefully argued case that infanticide by replacement males is a sexually selected adaptation in several species of monkeys and apes – sexual selection being the component of Darwinian selection that consists of differential access to mates. Hrdy's doctoral research was on the social behaviour of Hanuman langurs, a rather terrestrial species of Indian monkey mainly to be found in single-male, multiple-female troops. Langurs are like lions in that persistent social groups are matrilineal clans of closely related females and their young, whereas males are only temporary group members. Also similar to lion society is the fact that there are roving bachelors always eager to win breeding status in some troop of females, and that when a coup is successful, infants disappear soon after. This observation was not new with Hrdy. A previous observer, Yukimaru Sugiyama, had already concluded that male langurs killed infants after take-overs. But Hrdy spelled out the selectionist rationale, proposing that these disappearances were not incidental but functional: sexual selection would favour those males who disposed of their predecessors' nursing young and quickly got the females to work on the business of producing their own offspring.

Hrdy's sexually selected infanticide hypothesis initially drew a good deal of hostile fire. But in retrospect it is clear that the attacks had more to do with her critics' distaste for the facts than with flaws in Hrdy's evolutionary logic or in her evidence. The proposition that selection will favour infanticidal males over (hypothetical) non-infanticidal rivals is inescapable unless infanticide incurs offsetting costs, such as reduced mating opportunities or a risk of injuries inflicted by mothers defending their young. Hrdy's observations contained no reason to suppose that such costs existed.

To Robert Trivers, who served on Hrdy's dissertation committee and visited her field site, the sexually selected infanticide hypothesis was immediately compelling. In a highly influential paper published in 1972, Trivers had defined 'parental investment' to encompass everything that parents do that increases an individual offspring's expected fitness at some cost to the parent's capacity to invest its resources or efforts elsewhere, and he argued that this is the crucial quantity driving sexual selection. This perspective highlighted the fact that the energy and time expended in producing and rearing young, as well as risks incurred on their behalf, comprise a sort of resource, which, like any valuable resource, is sought after and contested. When one sex provides the bulk of parental investment, as females do in most mammals, then access to that investment – that is, access to the opportunity to be a genetic parent of the recipients of that investment – becomes the crucial limiting resource for the fitness – the reproductive success and genetic posterity – of individuals of the less investing sex.

In 1974, Trivers extended this 'economic' analysis with a remarkable exposition of 'parent–offspring conflict'. Parents face the problem of how best to allocate their parental investments both among extant young and between extant and potential future young, and Trivers showed that the ideal solution to this allocation problem from each youngster's perspective differs systematically from the parental ideal. These theoretical developments inspired researchers to try to measure parental investment and its allocation. One obvious hypothesis was that it would be allocated discriminatively with respect to cues indicative of whether the offspring was really the parent's own. When there were evolutionarily reliable indicators that a candidate for parental investment couldn't possibly be one's offspring, one might expect that parental psychologies should have evolved to eschew investment altogether. One such case arises in species with biparental care, when one partner dies or disappears while young are still dependent and is replaced by a step-parent.

CHAPTER 3

....

Human Stepfamilies

A surprisingly novel question

It was in the context of this sociobiological zeitgeist that we were first led to inquire to what extent Cinderella stories might be based in reality. We had completed our PhDs in animal behaviour in the early 1970s, and we had continued our studies of the social and sexual behaviour of desert rodents and monkeys post-doctorally. By about 1975, theories and research in our field might have inspired any animal behaviourist to wonder about step-parental affection and abuse.

Hrdy's observations and explanations of langur infanticide provided just one noteworthy example. Another was a paper published in *Science* in 1975 by ornithologist

Harry Power, who maintained that one should not expect birds who become the replacement mates of widowed parents to help feed their predecessors' off-spring. Power's presumption was that natural selection weeds out those who are willing to help raise others' young, because insofar as the basis of such 'altruism' is heritable, step-parental investment contributes to the replication and proliferation of the genes of rivals rather than the replication and proliferation of genes conducive to the development of the altruism. The logic parallels that used to explain infanticide by male langurs and lions, and Power's data on the behaviour of both naturally and experimentally widowed mountain bluebirds were mostly supportive of his predictions.

We had no particular interest in research on the human animal when, in 1976, we were among the cheerfully disputatious participants in a weekly evening seminar in California, working our way through Harvard entomologist Edward O. Wilson's *Sociobiology*. In his discussion of sexual selection, Wilson had written that the dramatic spectacle of combat over mating rights can engender the impression that same-sex competition is 'exclusively precopulatory in timing, ending with the act of insemination'. But not so, he maintained, for there are several modes of *post-copulatory* same-sex compe-tition, too, and he illustrated this competition by describ-ing sperm displacement devices (and counter-measures) in insects, induced abortion in mice, and what Hrdy was already calling sexually selected infanticide: 'Nomadic male langurs routinely kill all of the infants of a troop after they drive off the resident males; the usurpers quickly inseminate the females. A similar form of infanticide is perpetrated by male lions.' Wilson's presumption that these phenomena are routine and adaptive went beyond the evidence then available, but subsequent fieldwork has abundantly confirmed his interpretations.

It was in that *Sociobiology* seminar that a graduate student named Suzanne Weghorst raised the question: hey, what about human step-parents? Everyone knows the stereotype: they're hostile and 'wicked', right? Well, is there any truth behind this stereotype? Are stepchildren *really* disproportionately neglected and abused? It was an interesting question, but nobody in the room had any relevant expertise, so Ms Weghorst discovered the cost of speaking up in class. She was given the assignment of chasing down the relevant research studies and reporting back to the group.

What Suzanne had to report a week later was disappointing: she hadn't been able to find any evidence, one way or the other. Frankly, we were surprised. Fourteen years had passed since the American paediatrician Henry Kempe and his colleagues had proclaimed the existence of a 'battered-child syndrome', and child abuse had quickly achieved prominence in the media and in the public imagination. There was no shortage of research seeking to illuminate its correlates and causes. But no one seemed to have wondered about the mythic figure of the cruel step-parent. One American researcher, David Gil, had recorded that twenty-two per cent of a large sample of child abuse victims dwelt with one natural parent and one substitute parent, but he made nothing more of that raw fact. Gil did not remark on the need to determine to what degree that incidence might exceed chance expectation, nor did he raise the question of whether a high incidence of stepfamilies implies that step-relationship is itself germane and not simply an incidental correlate of some other risk factor such as poverty. Apparently, no other child abuse researcher had thought about genetic versus step-parenthood at all.

Gil's figure of twenty-two per cent sounded awfully high, but was it really so excessive, particularly at the socio-economic level from which the abuse cases were mainly drawn? We had no idea. It appeared that if we wanted to know the relevance of step-relationships to child maltreatment, we would have to do the research ourselves.

Stepfamily life

This is not to say that step-relationships were unstudied. There was already plenty of evidence that 'reconstituted' families were problematic. Anthropologist Meyer Fortes (1906–83) had demonstrated in the 1930s that American stepchildren left home at a younger age than their counterparts living with both genetic parents. Of course early departure might reflect the preferences of children, parents, or both, but regardless of whether stepchildren bolted or were pushed, the phenomenon probably entailed some parental withholding of investment relative to the investments made in children of the present marriage. In the 1950s, sociologist William C. Smith had assembled diverse evidence that step-parent/stepchild relationships are exceptionally conflictual, and in the 1960s, a massive study by Charles Bowerman and Donald Irish confirmed and extended Smith's claims.

We thought it particularly striking that researchers who deliberately recruited successfully functioning stepfamilies and who declared the debunking of Cinderella 'myths' to be one of their aims ended up telling much the same story. Lucile Duberman's 1975 monograph *The Reconstituted Family*, describing the results of an interview study of eighty-eight well-established, registered-marriage, predominantly middle-class stepfamilies in Cleveland, Ohio, is exemplary. Duberman was consistently upbeat about the prospects for workable and even satisfying steprelationships, but she had to acknowledge that 'There were very few stepparents who reported whole-hearted love for their stepchildren. Many expressed varying degrees of affection and others were optimistic about change in the future [p. 111].' Similarly, 'only a handful felt they were loved. However, this appears to have been the stepparental expectation and the stepparents seemed to be satisfied to get respect [p. 111].'

In sum, the research on stepfamily life that we were able to find in the 1970s seemed clear in its implications, even if the prevailing rhetoric about Cinderella 'myths' often tended to gainsay the actual findings. What we found then was what we still find in the much more abundant body of stepfamily research today: the central themes were the relatively loveless and unsatisfying quality of step-relationships, and how to cope with the ubiquitous aggravations and interpersonal conflicts of stepfamily life. Reading these studies, it seemed obvious to us that the conflicts and 'ambivalence' characteristic of step-relationships were the predictable consequences of putting people who had no human reason to love one another into a relationship that was structurally analogous to – and had to serve as a partial substitute for – the most intimate of loving relationships, namely that of parent and child. No one had yet attempted to compute rates of violent victimization in step-parent versus genetic parent homes, but our inclination to pursue the question was reinforced.

This inclination was further reinforced when we began to read anthropological reports about human behaviour in more traditional, non-state societies. Raymond Firth had written that in the Pacific island paradise of Tikopia, a man who acquired a wife who was already a mother would be forthcoming about his unwillingness to invest in a predecessor's child, declaiming 'Who is this child for whom I must fetch food from the woods?' and demanding that the child be either fostered out or destroyed. This was not an isolated case. Among the Yanomamä Indians of Venezuela, for example, men who abducted the mothers of infants reportedly insisted that those children be killed. And of course parallels also abound in the sagas, epics, and biblical accounts of Eurasian history.

In 1976, a study of marital conflict provided new

evidence that even where the role of step-parent is accepted rather than refused, step-parental investment remains a contested issue. Louise Messinger asked remarried Canadians with children from previous marriages to rank the areas of 'overt conflict' in each of their marriages. 'Children' and 'money' topped the list for the remarriages, but were hardly ever mentioned for the failed first marriages, and it was clear that these two ostensibly distinct issues were really one and the same: the mother wanted more of the stepfather's resources invested in her children than he was inclined to contribute.

In 1977, Gary Becker and colleagues published what they called an 'economic analysis of marital instability' based on a large body of American demographic data. What their analyses seemed to show is that the presence of children of the current marriage has the effect of reducing the divorce rate for first and subsequent marriages alike, whereas the presence of children of former marriages raises it. From this and other evidence on marriageability and resource allocation, Becker – who was subsequently awarded the Nobel Prize for extending economic theory and analysis into family affairs – inferred that one's own genetic children must be considered to have positive utility in their own right, rather than being valued as means to the end of wealth accrual, whereas stepchildren have negative utility.

The emerging picture made sense to us as evolutionists. Having children of one's own and raising them have always been the primary routes by which women and men attain genetic posterity (Darwinian fitness). Insofar as motives and emotions have evolved to promote fitness, we might therefore expect children to be sources of parental harmony rather than discord. Anything that helps or hurts a given child's well-being has the same impact on the fitness of both parents, with the result that mother's and father's evaluations of various hypothetical futures are likely to converge. A mated pair's aspirations and fears are apt to be more similar the greater their investment of time and energy and love in their joint project. But whereas children of the present union facilitate consensus on the crucial question of how the couple's resources should be allocated, children from former unions could be expected to have exactly the opposite effect.

Evolutionary reasoning and the evidence were in accord. It seemed clear that assuming step-parental duties must typically be perceived as a cost rather than a benefit in remarriage negotiations, and that the magnitude of that step-parental obligation must be contested and not infrequently resented.

CHAPTER 4

....

The Truth about Cinderella

The first test: US child abuse reports

Our first attempt to measure the impact of step-relation-ships on the incidence of child abuse made use of a data archive maintained by the American Humane Association (AHA). This organization had assumed the role of central repository for legally mandated child abuse reports in most of the United States, and had a computer file containing tens of thousands of case reports. For each victimized child, the data included basic demographic facts about victim and (alleged) perpetrator, details of the nature of the abuse, the relationship between the victim and the persons *in loco parentis*, and whether the case had been 'validated' in some sort of follow-up investigation beyond the initial report.

To compute the age-specific rates of abuse of step-children *versus* others, we also needed data on the living arrangements of children in the population at large. This information was elusive. The US census of population did not distinguish among genetic, adoptive and step-parenthood, and all we could find were estimates based on limited surveys, which almost certainly exaggerated the prevalence of step-relationships because of some unrealistic assumptions that had been made to derive the estimates. But we used them anyway, since they made our comparisons 'conservative': an overestimation of the number of stepfamilies in the population should lead us to underestimate their maltreatment rates and make it more difficult to demonstrate an elevation. But the elevation of risk was dramatic none the less: according to our calculations, a child under three years of age who lived with one genetic parent and one step-parent in the United States in 1976 was about seven times more likely (the 'odds ratio' in epidemiological parlance) to become a validated child-abuse case in the AHA records than one who dwelt with two genetic parents.

There are a number of reasons to be cautious about interpreting this sort of comparison. One is the possibility of biased detection or reportage. Suppose that you lived next door to a child who exhibited recurrent, suspicious bruising, and that you (like everyone else) were familiar with the stereotype of step-parental cruelty. Isn't it possible that your likelihood of assuming the worst and calling a child protection agency might be affected by knowing that the man in the house was a stepfather?

Biases of this sort could create the appearance of differential risk where none actually exists. However, there was strong evidence that this was not what was happening in the AHA data. We reasoned that as the severity of child abuse increases, up to the extreme of lethal battering, it should be increasingly unequivocal, so distortions due to biased detection and reportage should diminish. But as we made our abuse criteria increasingly stringent and narrowed the sample down to the most unmistakable cases, the over-representation of stepfamilies did not diminish. Quite the contrary, in fact. By the time we had reduced the cases under consideration from the full file of 87,789 validated maltreatment reports to the 279 fatal child-abuse cases, the estimated rates in step-parent-plus-genetic-parent households had grown to approximately *one hundred times* greater than in two-genetic-parent households.

There could be no doubt that the excess risk in stepfamilies was both genuine and huge. But whether it really had anything to do with step-relationship *per se* was not necessarily resolved. Perhaps living with a step-parent was associated with some other factor of more direct relevance.

One obvious candidate for such a 'confounding' factor is poverty. If step-parenthood is especially prevalent among the poor (which seemed plausible since marital stability was known to be correlated with income) and if the poor also have high rates of detected child abuse (which they do), then differentials of the sort we had observed might be expected even if step-parent and genetic-parent homes were identically risky within any particular income level. But this initially plausible hypothesis was rejected, for it turned out that the distribution of family incomes in step-parent homes in the United States was virtually identical to that in two-genetic-parent homes. Low-income families were indeed over-represented in the AHA dataset, but the association between abuse and poverty was independent of (was 'orthogonal' to) the association between abuse and step-relationship.

Further research in Canada

We published our US results in a brief journal article in 1980 and in greater detail in 1981, and we turned our attentions elsewhere. But we were never entirely happy with our initial study, for several reasons. The population-at-large estimates were questionable; the 'abuse' criteria were not necessarily consistent from state to state; and the data were inadequate for testing additional 'confound' hypotheses other than poverty. So a few years later, having moved back home to Canada, we decided to conduct a better controlled, smaller-scale, local study of the same issues.

The regional municipality of Hamilton-Wentworth, where we live, is the centre of Canada's steel industry and home to almost half-a-million souls. The local child-protection agencies provided us with information about all cases severe enough to have warranted filing a report with the provincial child-abuse registry, and we surveyed the relevant population-at-large ourselves. About one in every 3,000 Hamilton pre-schoolers residing with both genetic parents was reported to the Ontario child-abuse registry in 1983. The corresponding rate for those living with a step-parent plus a genetic parent was about one in seventy-five, hence forty times greater. This odds ratio was smaller than that which we had found for lethal abuse in the United States, but larger than that for all child abuse, perhaps because the case criterion in our Hamilton study was of intermediate severity.

The odds ratio of abuse risk in Hamilton stepfamilies versus genetic-parent families was substantial for children of all ages, but it declined steadily from forty for pre-schoolers to about ten for teenaged victims. A similar trend had also been apparent in our US study, and we saw an important implication. Most of those who had written on stepfamily conflicts apparently believed that the problems are primarily created by obstreperous adolescents rejecting their custodial parents' new mates; but this could hardly be correct if the elevation of risk from step-parents was maximal for infants. Our hypothesis that the more basic problem is the adult's resentment of pseudo-parental obligation fits the facts much better.

Another consistent result from both studies was that excess risk in stepfamilies spanned the gamut of 'abuse' from baby batterings to sexual molestation of older children. This also reinforced our conviction that we were looking at what might be called a 'reverse assay' of parental love. A paucity of heartfelt, individualized concern for the welfare of a child in one's care would seem likely to raise the incidence of any sort of misuse.

Still another consistent result was that step-parent-hood's impact was statistically independent of poverty's additional effects. Family size, which we had not been able to assess in the US study, proved to be another independent risk factor. Maternal youth was yet another. Evolutionary theories of maternal investment had suggested to us that older mothers might be more selfless than younger. As menopause approaches, investing in the children you already have has less and less negative impact on your expected future reproduction. Evolved maternal psychologies might be expected to reflect this reliable feature of women's life histories. We therefore anticipated that abuse risk would decline steadily as a function of the mother's age at the child's birth, and this expectation was upheld. All in all, although several additional risk factors were identified, step-parenthood held its place as the most important predictor, and its influence was scarcely diminished when the statistical impacts of all the other risk factors were controlled.

It warrants repeating that even severe child abuse is vulnerable to detection biases, but that these biases presumably shrink as the case criterion becomes more extreme. At the limit, we can be reasonably confident that child murders are usually detected and recorded. Admittedly, some failures to help a newborn live may escape detection and some deliberate smotherings may be successfully disguised as 'sudden infant deaths', but there is no reason to suppose that these are numerous, and in any event, the brutal assaultive homicides that are motivated by rage or hatred cannot be disguised in this way. So after completing our study of registered child-abuse cases in Hamilton, we undertook analyses of homicides, using an official government archive containing data on all homicides known to Canadian police departments. Once again, just as we had found in the United States, the over-representation of step-parents as perpetrators of child murder in Canada proved to be even more extreme than their over-representation as perpetrators of non-lethal child abuse. As we reported in an article in *Science* in 1988, a co-residing step-parent was approximately seventy times more likely to kill a child under two years of age than was a co-residing genetic parent, and this odds ratio was still about fifteen for teenage victims.

The emerging cross-national evidence

We now know that the story in Great Britain is much the same as in North America: step-parents are hugely over-represented as perpetrators of registered child abuse and even more hugely as child murderers. According to a report produced by the National Society for the Prevention of Cruelty to Children, entitled *Child Abuse Trends in England & Wales 1983–1987*, thirty-two per cent of the 4,037 nationally registered victims of intentionally inflicted physical injuries in that five-year period lived with one natural parent and one substitute parent, whereas a random sample of children with the same age distribution from the population-at-large would have yielded only three per cent. Unlike the situation in

North America, stepfamilies in the United Kingdom tend to have slightly lower incomes than two-genetic-parent families, so that the excess of step-parents may in this case be partly an artifact of economic differences. However, when family income was controlled, children in stepfamilies remained nineteen times more likely to be registered as victims of non-accidental physical injuries inflicted by caretakers than were children from two-genetic-parent homes.

As for child murder, there was one relevant report dating from before we began our own research. In 1973, forensic psychiatrist P. D. Scott had summarized information on a sample of 'fatal battered-baby cases' perpetrated in anger by British men *in loco paternis*, and despite the fact that the victims averaged just fifteen months of age, fifteen of the twenty-nine killers – fifty-two per cent – were stepfathers. Scott did not attempt to convert these numbers to rates or odds ratios, but relevant population-at-large information can now be derived from a major study of a cohort born in 1970, and it turns out that fewer than one per cent of a sample of children with the same age distribution as the fatally battered babies would be expected to have had a stepfather. In this case, the odds ratio for this particular kind of lethal assault by stepfathers versus genetic fathers was approximately 150.

It seemed likely, both from the evidence of these baby batterings and from our evolution-minded hypothesis about step-parental reluctance and resentment, that excess risk from step-parents might be especially severe with regard to angry outbursts. Little children *are* annoying, after all: they cry and soil themselves and sometimes refuse to be consoled. A caretaker with a heartfelt, individualized love for a squalling baby is motivated to tenderly alleviate its distress, but a caretaker who is simply playing the part without emotional commitment – and who might even prefer that the child had never been born – is apt to respond rather differently.

Filicides by genetic parents certainly occur. In absolute numbers, they actually exceed the cases perpetrated by step-parents, although the latter occur at much higher per capita rates. But the cases are not similar. The Home Office maintains a case-by-case data archive on homicides in England and Wales, similar to the Canadian archive mentioned above. Although the information in these archives is sparse, consisting solely of numerical codings of a number of standard variables, it still proves revealing as regards the characteristics of killings by genetic *versus* step-parents. Confining our inquiry to cases in which the victims were less than five years of age, in order to exclude all possibility of mutual combat or self-defence on the killer's part, we find a similar pattern in both countries: about eighty per cent of homicidal stepfathers are found to have battered, kicked or bludgeoned their victims to death, whereas the majority of those who killed their genetic offspring did so by less assaultive means. Moreover, in the course of seventeen years of Canadian data and fourteen years of British data, seventy-three of the 390 men who killed their own children did so in the context of a successfully completed suicide, compared to just three of the 197 who killed stepchildren. There is also evidence that diagnosed psychiatric conditions are prevalent among those who kill their genetic children, but not among those who kill stepchildren. In summary, filicidal genetic parents of both sexes are often deeply depressed, are likely to kill the children while they sleep, and may even construe murder-suicide as a humane act of rescue from a cruel world, whereas homicidal step-parents are seldom suicidal and typically manifest their antipathy to their victims in the relative brutality of their lethal acts.

In recent years, diverse strands of evidence from a variety of countries have shown that step-parental mis-treatment of children is widespread. In New South Wales, Australia, for example, stepfathers have been found to be even more extremely over-represented as the perpetrators of baby batterings than in Canada, the United States, and Great Britain. In Finland, a 1996 report of a questionnaire study of 9,000 fifteen-year-olds indicated that 3·7 per cent of girls currently living with a stepfather claimed that he had abused them sexually, compared to 0·2 per cent of those living with their genetic fathers. (The only case of 'mother-son' sexual contact in this study, incidentally, involved a fifteen-year-old boy and his twenty-six-year-old stepmother; in contrast to the girls, all of whom found sexual contact with stepfathers or fathers aversive, 'the boy described the experience as positive'.) Korean schoolchildren living with either a stepfather or a stepmother claim to be beaten at very much higher rates than their two-genetic-parent classmates. Recent studies in Hong Kong, Nigeria, Japan and Trinidad paint similar pictures.

It has also become clear that the hazards associated with being a stepchild are not a novel product of the modern age. Using historical archives from the seventeenth to the nineteenth century, the German anthropologist Eckart Voland has shown that Cinderella stories were more than mere fairy tales for European peasants. Voland found that the age-specific mortality of premodern Friesian children was elevated in the aftermath of the death of either parent and, more tellingly, that the risk of death was further elevated if the surviving parent remarried.

In the face-to-face societies of our ancestors, powerful central authority and social services beyond kin assistance were non-existent, and the situation for stepchildren was probably even worse than in peasant societies. According to one study of contemporary South American hunter-gatherers, the Ache of Paraguay, forty-three per cent of children brought up by a mother and stepfather died before their fifteenth birthdays, compared to nineteen per cent of those brought up by two genetic parents; apparently, deaths by assault and deaths due to deprivation of adequate care were both elevated. Hunter-gatherer societies provide our best model of the social circumstances in which the human animal evolved and to which our psyches are adapted. We hypothesize that it has been a general feature of such societies that stepchildren are variously disadvantaged – as they are among the Ache – and we know of no contrary evidence.

CHAPTER 5

··

Parental Priorities

Allocating limited parental resources

After all these sorry statistics, it is perhaps important to stress the other side of the coin. Human beings are not like langurs or lions. We know that 'sexually selected infanticide' is not a human adaptation because men, unlike male langurs and lions, do not routinely, efficiently dispose of their predecessors' young. Stepfathers are very much more likely to inflict non-lethal abuse than to kill, and such abuse is obviously not a 'well-designed' means to hasten the production of one's own children nor even to reduce the costs of step-parental investment. Child abuse must therefore be considered a non-adaptive or maladaptive byproduct of the evolved psyche's functional organization, rather than an adaptation in its own right. Moreover, because of the complex social life of the human animal, which includes reputations and retribution, those who assault or kill children flirt with disaster. All told, we see little reason to imagine that the average reproductive benefits of killing stepchildren would ever have outweighed the average costs enough to select for specifically infanticidal inclinations.

Quite unlike the situation in langurs or lions, human stepfamilies exist in all societies, and most stepchildren survive them. Many, perhaps most, step-parents derive some pleasure from helping raise their partners' children, and many, perhaps most, stepchildren are better off than if their parents had remained single. However, although sexually selected infanticide is clearly not a human adaptation, discriminative parental solicitude just as clearly is, and the discrimination is not simply a matter of responding to the 'cute' cues of a generic healthy child.

Because parental love carries with it an onerous commitment, it would be strange if merely pairing up with someone who already had a dependent child were sufficient to fully engage the evolved psychology of parental feeling. And it is not sufficient. Step-parents do not, on average, feel the same child-specific love and commitment as genetic parents, and therefore do not reap the same emotional rewards from unreciprocated 'parental' investment. Enormous differentials in the risk of violence are just one, particularly dramatic, consequence of this predictable difference in feelings.

The Darwinian process favours attributes that contribute to their own proliferation relative to alternatives. That's *all* it favours, all it *can* favour. It follows that the behavioural control mechanisms of any creature – its motives, emotions, attentional priorities, and so forth – have been shaped by the process of natural selection to be effective means to the ends of personal and kin reproductive success.

In this light, we may expect the psychology of parental solicitude in any species to be designed to allocate parental investment discriminatively, in ways that will promote the individual parent's genetic posterity (inclusive fitness). Successful discrimination of one's own offspring from unrelated young is not the only allocation problem facing parental investors, but it can be a crucial one. Indiscriminate allocation of parental benefits without regard to cues of actual parentage would be an evolutionary anomaly.

A famous allegation of just such indiscriminacy concerns the Mexican free-tailed bat. This species roosts in dark caves in aggregations that can number in the millions. Within hours of giving birth, females hang their singleton pups from the roof, in the midst of a wriggling, crawling mass of several thousand pups per square metre, and go out to forage. Noting these facts and having demonstrated that pups would seize the nipple of any female held near them, and that the females would then accept them, researchers operating within the greater-goodist paradigm of the early 1960s had concluded that the colony of females constituted an 'anonymous dairy herd'.

This conclusion demands our scepticism. The mother bat suffers both energy depletion and predation risk in order to gather enough insects to deliver milk equivalent to sixteen per cent of her total body weight each day. If milk were truly a communal resource, selection would surely favour the female who deposits her pup in the care of the dairy herd, dries up, and opts out, with the result that lactation could not be 'evolutionarily stable'. And yet costly lactation persists. Doubting the dairy herd theory for this reason, Gary McCracken and collaborators began analysing the genetic make-up of mothers and infants in the field in the late 1970s, and they found that while mismatches indeed occurred, the great majority of nursing pairs consisted of a mother and her own infant. Exactly how the mother bats go about locating their pups in the chaotic cave crèche has turned out to involve exquisitely discriminative use of both sound and smell before the pup is allowed to attach to the nipple, but if the mother's normal pup-locating strategy is circumvented, as it was in the early experiments, then she will indeed give suck to whomever reaches her breast.

The environment of evolutionary adaptiveness

We refer to the mother bat's 'strategy' for locating her own pup because she possesses abilities and performs a sequence of actions that are well organized to achieve that end. But the fact that she can be fooled illustrates the point that 'strategy' is a metaphor. Motives and emotions and sensory abilities function to bring about certain fitness-promoting outcomes because they have evolved by selection, but their functionality does not imply that the animal recognizes its own 'objectives'.

Thus, refining this chapter's initial claims, we should say that parental psyches are designed to allocate parental efforts in ways that would have promoted parental fitness in the species' ancestral environment of evolutionary adaptiveness (EEA), that is the environment within which the relevant history of natural selection occurred. Any population's contemporary environment includes consistent, long-standing features to which the animals are evolutionarily adapted (the attributes of the EEA), but it also includes relative novelties to which they are not.

In the domain of parental discrimination, different species possess different abilities, and the differences become intelligible when we consider the differences in their EEAs. Guillemots ('murres' in Canada) are marine birds who lay their eggs on rock ledges only a few centimetres from nesting neighbours. They recognize their newly hatched chicks and even their eggs on the basis of individual markings, and they reject any unrelated chicks or eggs that somehow turn up in the nest uninvited. The closely related razorbill nests more dispersedly in the same habitat, so that although the two species' EEAs are similar in many particulars, the razorbill's EEA entails no risk of spontaneous transpositions of neighbouring young. In consequence, the razorbill lacks the specialized discriminative abilities of the guillemot and is oblivious to experimental cross-fostering of eggs and hatchlings.

Similarly, some species of swallows nest in colonies while others nest dispersedly. Only the colonial species incur risk of misdirecting their parental investments in nature, both because newly volant young sometimes return to the wrong nest and because fledged young, who are still being fed by their parents, gather in crèches. Again, adults of the colonial species recognize their own young but adults of the more dispersed species do not, and in this case, relevant adaptations in both the young and the parents have been identified. The voices of colonial species chicks are intrinsically more variable and distinguishable than those of the dispersed nesters' chicks, and the auditory discrimination abilities of the colonial species parents are better developed than those of their dispersed species counterparts.

The evolutionist's expectation that parental solicitude will be individualized stands in contrast to the dominant model of maternal motivation in physiological psychology. In this field, maternal inclination is treated as a motivational state of the mother that is non-specific with respect to its object. This conception is a result of happenstance: maternal solicitude is indeed remarkably indiscriminate in the laboratory rat, a species that has dominated research for no other reason than its convenience. A lab rat who has been rendered 'maternal' by experience or by hormone manipulation will behave maternally towards standard 'stimulus pups' placed in her cage, and even to pups of other species, for essentially the same reason that Mexican free-tailed bats nursed unrelated pups in the early, misleading experiments:

because her defences against such parasitism have been bypassed. But in nature, burrow-dwelling rodents such as rats defend their nest sites aggressively, so that alien young in the nest are not a problem. After a couple of weeks, when the growing pups are becoming mobile and mix-ups are an imminent possibility, mothers come to recognize their pups as individuals and will no longer accept fostered young.

In mammals who do not sequester their young – such as colonial bats and seals and herd-living hoofed mammals whose young are up and walking within minutes of birth – mothers establish individualized bonds with their young immediately after birth, and then reject and even attack unrelated milk thieves of the same age and infantile appeal as their own young, while remaining fully 'maternal'. In short, there is nothing magical about discriminative allocation of parental investment to one's own offspring. It depends on evolved tendencies to attend and respond to specific cues that helped parents make such discriminations in the EEA, and evolutionarily novel manipulations of the environment can circumvent it.

Presumptive parenthood

In species in which fertilization occurs inside the female's body, a mother can inspect and learn to recognize her own young at birth. But a male must rely on other cues if he is going to favour those young who are really his own. Songbirds that were once considered 'monogamous' have turned out to have varying incidences of 'extra-pair paternity', and in some species, males adjust the effort that they expend feeding the chicks in response to cues of such cuckoldry. These cues include the proximity of rival males during his mate's fertile period (weeks before the chicks have hatched and are to be fed); whether neighbouring males are more or less attractive than the resident male himself; and what percentage of that fertile period his mate spent out of his sight.

In principle, there are two broad classes of paternity cues available to doubtful fathers: those reflecting the likelihood of female infidelity around the time of conception and those manifested by the offspring themselves, who may or may not resemble the putative father or his relatives. Remarkably, no non-human animal has yet been shown capable of using these latter cues of resemblance for the purpose of adaptively modulating paternal investment. But people certainly can do this – perhaps especially with the assistance of interested, observant relatives – and it turns out that parents and relatives on both the maternal and paternal sides are much more interested in babies' resemblances to the father's side than the mother's, even if paternity doubt is not an (overt) issue. Whether human fathers then adjust their investments in relation to resemblance is still unknown.

An obvious evolutionary psychological hypothesis is that the child's resemblance to the investing parent will influence paternal affection more than it affects maternal affection, since resemblance was a potentially informative paternity cue in the human EEA, while maternity was not in doubt. No one yet knows whether this is true. But if it is true, we predict that the discrimination will be a relatively 'automatic' response that operates apart from consciously articulatable beliefs and knowledge, and we therefore predict that the affections of adoptive fathers – who know full well that their children are not their genetic offspring – will be more strongly influenced by apparent similarities to themselves than will be the case with adoptive mothers. The reason we are bothering to mention these untested ideas here is to re-emphasize an important general point: hypothesizing a complex evolved psychology of parenthood, designed by natural selection to bring about fitness-promoting allocations of parental investment in the EEA, does not necessarily imply that such allocations are goals that the actor is aware of and can pursue with behavioural flexibility in novel situations.

The suggestion is often made that if stepfamily conflicts and violence are indeed the byproducts of an evolutionarily structured discriminative parental solicitude, as we have argued, then adoptive children should suffer similar or greater risks. But it is not that simple. Adoptive parents are eager to adopt, are screened for suitability, and have the option of changing their minds (an option that they exercise surprisingly often). How adoptive parenthood compares to relevant aspects of the EEA is a complex topic in need of investigation, but it is clear that the contemporary practice of adoption by unrelated persons attempting to simulate the experience of genetic families is a modern novelty. Step-parenthood is not. Remarriage and its attendant opportunities and pressures to invest in one's new mate's extant children have been prevalent features of the human EEA for as long as men and women have formed parentally investing couples.

CHAPTER 6

....

Cinderella Denied

A distasteful discovery?

Our research on family violence has not been confined to comparisons of genetic versus step-relationships. After all, if extreme violence is the tip of the iceberg of interpersonal conflicts, then it may provide a window on the conflicts characteristic of any close relationship. For example, we have discovered striking demographic patterns in the risk that a man will kill his wife. Women in common-law unions are killed at higher rates than those in registered marriages; risk declines with the duration of the marriage and (at least partially independently) with the wife's increasing age; a large age disparity between marital partners is a major risk factor; and women with children sired by previous partners incur greatly elevated rates of murder by their current partners. These patterns of homicide are for the most part duplicated when one looks at the much more frequent phenomenon of non-lethal wife assault, and are readily interpreted as simply the most extreme manifestations of patterns of marital conflict.

As far as we know, these striking patterns of differential risk have never been called 'controversial'. We have not been met with outrage and denial when we have reported them. But the fact that step-parents abuse and kill children at vastly higher rates than genetic parents is somehow a different story: here, although the risk differentials are even larger and more extensively documented, the findings are routinely labelled 'controversial' in media reports, and are sometimes even indignantly dismissed as incredible. There is something about the association between step-parenthood and child maltreatment that appears to be uniquely unpalatable, and we have witnessed some curious attempts to make it vanish.

Family violence researchers Jean Giles-Sims and David Finkelhor, for example, began a 1984 paper that reviewed the already considerable evidence as follows: 'There is an often repeated presumption that children are at increased risk of abuse at the hands of stepparents. This paper tries to initiate a more formal examination of the evidence.' Having thus gratuitously implied that prior studies were in some unspecified sense prejudicial and flawed, Giles-Sims and Finkelhor reported their own findings: step-parents were identified as perpetrators in a whopping twenty-four per cent of all child-abuse cases in a large US 'National Incidence Study'. The authors then noted the widely cited estimate by US Census demographer Paul Glick that ten per cent of US children under eighteen years of age lived with a step-parent, and continued with a lengthy argument to the effect that Glick's estimate might be low and hence that it is still impossible to know whether twenty-four per cent constitutes an excess.

This argument was remarkable not only because it ignored the fact that the abuse victims were much younger on average than the group to which Glick's estimate applied, and therefore much less likely to have step-parents, but also because published survey data had already confirmed what we had long maintained, namely that Glick's estimate of ten per cent (which was based on several false assumptions such as that all children born before a remarriage was registered were stepchildren) was actually too high. Giles-Sims and Finkelhor furthermore proposed, in words implying that the point was novel, that even if twenty-four per cent does exceed the prevalence of step-parents in the population-at-large, their over-representation might disappear if socio-economic status were statistically controlled. This, too, was a remarkable argument, given that this possibility had been raised and disposed of in papers that they cited.

Perhaps Giles-Sims and Finkelhor's reluctance to believe their own evidence that step-parents are over-represented as child abusers was still a tenable stance in 1984. By 1991, it certainly was not. Several published surveys had shown that popular claims about the large and rapidly growing prevalence of stepfamilies were greatly exaggerated and had provided a basis for accurate estimation of the more modest numbers of children living with step-parents in Canada, the United Kingdom, and the United States. The same surveys had also shown that the incidence of step-relationships was not importantly confounded with income, although there was some relationship in the United Kingdom.

There was now a wealth of evidence, from a number of countries, that step-parents were massively over-represented as perpetrators of both sexual and physical abuse. Moreover, the Canadian, British and American data all showed that this excess was most extreme precisely with respect to the most extreme and unequivocal sorts of child abuse, namely fatal batterings, refuting any suggestion that the abundance of step-parents might represent nothing more than biases in the labelling of ambiguous or marginal cases. Still another 'confound' hypothesis, namely the idea that the abuse differences might reflect an excess of indiscriminately violent personalities in remarriages, had been disposed of by demonstrations that mistreatment in stepfamilies was usually discriminatively targeted at the stepchild while the abuser's own children in the same household were well treated, just like Cinderella and her stepsisters. Our interpretations might be controversial, but we could not imagine how the fact of excess risk in stepfamilies could be called into question. It seems that we were not imaginative enough.

The counter-evidence

In 1991, the reality of excess risk in stepfamilies was indeed called into question by perhaps the most prominent family violence researcher in America, Richard Gelles. One prong of his attack was an empirical study co-authored with John Harrop, using data from a telephone survey conducted in 1985. Respondents had been asked a series of questions such as whether they had 'slapped' certain family members (considered one by one) within the last year, had 'punched' them, had 'used a knife or gun on' them, and so forth, when they 'had a disagreement or were angry with them'. It will probably come as no surprise that the 117 step-parents who did not hang up on this unsolicited call from a stranger and completed the interview were no more likely to profess that they had assaulted the children under their care than were genetic parents.

To Gelles and Harrop's way of thinking, this was the first test of the controversial hypothesis of differential abuse 'that has met the normal standards of social scientific evidence'. They acknowledged the existence of a wealth of evidence that step-relationships entail increased risk, but considered it all to be tainted evidence, subject to 'the confounds of using official child-abuse report data'. Their uniquely contrary result, on the other hand, was likely to be uniquely valid because the data were collected in a study of a 'large nationally representative sample' that was 'free' of such biases. (Incidentally, more recent evidence from the US

National Survey of Families and Households indicates that
even in such interviews, step-parents do report striking
the children substantially more often than genetic parents
if the question is framed in the more defensible language
of 'discipline' rather than with reference to 'disagreement' and 'anger').

In another widely cited 1991 paper, Gelles proposed
that our analyses of 1976 American Humane Association
(AHA) data might have been 'flawed and biased' by
virtue of our having compared abuse rates in step-parent
versus genetic parent households without consideration
of whether the step-parent was the identified abuser.
This argument was supported by reference to an unpub-
lished study in which Catherine Malkin and Michael
Lamb had analysed a later (1984) set of such perpetrator–
victim relationship data from the same source, and had,
in Gelles's words, 'failed to find that stepparents were
more likely to abuse their offspring than biological
parents'. Malkin and Lamb's paper was not published
until 1994, and anyone who troubled to check it against
Gelles's citation must have been puzzled: the analysis
merely compared the proportionate representation of
step-parents in one category of abuse cases versus
another, and contained no estimates of abuse rates at the
hands of step-parents versus genetic parents at all. Malkin
and Lamb did indeed seem to imagine that their analyses
constituted some sort of failure to replicate our results,
despite the fact that thirty-nine per cent of their victims
living in 'two-parent' homes dwelt with step-parents
(the expected value for a population sample with the

same age distribution would have been less than five per cent), and despite the fact that step-parents were disproportionately the identified abusers even within their sample. And they did indeed seem to imply that analysis by perpetrator eliminated some unspecified artifact produced by our household analyses, despite the fact that analysing by perpetrator actually produces much *greater* step-parent/genetic parent odds ratios than our more conservative analysis by household.

Ironically, the proportion of AHA abuse reports that involved step-parents had actually increased between 1976 and 1984, and so had the absolute and relative differences in abuse rates between step-parent families and genetic-parent families. Moreover, there was no statistical rationale for suggesting that rate differences could have been spuriously produced by analysing the data at the household level, not even in principle. Nevertheless, this incoherent claim continues to be parroted as a reason to doubt the evidence.

Gelles and Harrop's claim that confessions of child abuse to a telephone interviewer have greater validity than the injuries and deaths of battered babies has been endorsed by the Council on Scientific Affairs of the American Medical Association (AMA). In a report on 'Adolescents as victims of family violence', published in the AMA's flagship journal *JAMA* in 1993 with the express goal of helping family physicians identify abuse victims, this prestigious panel asserted that 'Families with stepparents have been reported to be at higher risk for both physical and sexual abuse of adolescents and younger children. However, several authors have argued that methodological flaws and the possibility of bias in official reports raise questions about these findings. Official reports are analysed using households as units of comparison and do not identify the relationship of the perpetrator to the child. Therefore, it is unclear if step-parents are more likely to perpetrate abuse than are genetic parents. In addition, agencies may be more likely to classify cases as abusive if a stepparent is present due to assumptions about differences between a child's relationship with a genetic and nongenetic caretaker.' In accordance with this reasoning, the report's recommendations, which were adopted by the House of Delegates of the AMA at its annual meeting in 1992 and which included a list of abuse risk factors that family physicians should screen for, do not mention step-parenthood at all.

The AMA's contentions that perpetrators have not been identified and that biased reporting might account for the findings are of course false, but the Council on Scientific Affairs makes no reference to the research literature dealing with these claims. In fact, the report contains no citation of *any* of the research demonstrating differential rates of lethal and non-lethal abuse at the hands of step-parents versus genetic parents, a remarkable omission given that readers are assured that 'This report reflects the scientific literature as of March 1992', and given that such research had been appearing in scientific journals for more than a decade. As for the claim that 'methodological flaws' had been pointed out by 'several authors', the AMA report provides a single citation: Gelles and Harrop.

Can we help?

As we noted before, there is a substantial body of stepfamily research that has nothing to do with child abuse. But it has everything to do with the fact that conflicts are rampant. Study after study has shown that marital happiness is reduced in stepfamilies, and that step-parent and stepchild alike view their relationships as less loving and as less dependable sources of material and emotional support than genetic parent-child relationships. There is also a wealth of evidence that parental investment is withheld from stepchildren. Many studies have found that the parents in stepfamilies look forward to happier days once the children leave, and that stepchildren indeed leave home at a relatively young age. In a recent study of homeless adolescents aged fifteen to seventeen in New York, stepchildren were hugely over-represented, and routinely claimed to have been abused in the parental home or 'pushed out' or both. In Britain, the *National Child Development Study* demonstrated that both the genetic and the step-parent express low aspirations for the children's education in step-parent homes, lower even than the aspirations of single mothers, and that the children's own aspirations follow suit. In the United States, it has been found that those stepchildren who do manage to enter college receive less parental help with their tuition than those coming from genetic-parent homes with the same family income.

The picture is consistent and unsurprising. The proverbial man on the street might have guessed these things. But the researchers who have documented these facts generally try to steer wide of any implication that the stepfamily is an inferior vehicle for rearing children and finding marital bliss. Why? Perhaps the main reason is that the writers feel that stepfamily life is hard enough, without adding to the stigma. Duberman's 1975 classic *The Reconstituted Family* set the tone: after reviewing evidence that the relationships between stepchildren and step-parents are 'considerably less harmonious than between children and parents in primary homes', she added, 'This author feels that many of the problems are generated by the Cinderella myth, and that the myth does not square with the facts [p. 51]'. More recently, ostensibly scientific reviews of the empirical literature on stepfamily dynamics have evaluated the papers not with respect to the adequacy of their methods, but with respect to whether they adequately accentuate the positive by stressing such 'stepfamily strengths' as the fact that stepchildren 'have two sets of parents to whom they can turn for help' or that stepfamilies provide 'valuable experience of complex social forms'.

The prevalence of such vacuous pap is largely a result of well-intentioned efforts to help stepfamilies cope. But it is also a product of a naive psychology. The predominant conceptual framework in this area is 'role theory': parenthood is considered one role and step-parenthood another. The role concept has usefully directed attention to the importance of 'scripts' and social learning, but it is at best a limited metaphor that has diverted attention from the motivational and emotional aspects of the social psyche. A role can be filled by any competent actor who has learned the part. But there is a great deal more to social action than knowing your lines. Parents care deeply for their children's well-being and future prospects, but human cares are absent from role theorists' explanations of human action.

Several researchers have proposed that the problem with being a step-parent is that the role is 'incompletely institutionalized', and that step-parents therefore don't know what they are supposed to do. Some step-parents do indeed describe their anguish and inconsistent behaviour as a sort of perplexity, but this is surely a sign of internal motivational conflicts rather than of the absence of a script. People are ambivalent when they have conflicting desires and when they feel that they must do what they don't really want to do.

In Carol Shields's novel *The Republic of Love*, a thirty-five-year-old woman phones her gynaecologist mother to say that she has broken up with her latest boyfriend. In the midst of a rambling reply, the supportive but disappointed mother says, 'We just thought that eventually you'd get the urge to start a family, you're both so crazy about kids, and you've no idea how different it is with kids of your own, you love them ten times more than you love other people's. It takes people by surprise how much love they have stored up. Young mothers are always telling me that, how they actually fall in love with their babies. Fall in love, that's how they phrase it . . .'

This fictitious gynaecologist's claims are abundantly supported by research, and they are hardly news to ordinary people. But family-relations researchers who consider parenthood a mere 'role' seem to be unaware that parental love is individualized. When stepfamily conflicts are too conspicuous to ignore, they are blamed on such irrelevant matters as the fact that the adults internalized different models of how children should be reared in their own natal families, indeed on almost anything other than the painful possibility that love cannot simply be willed and many step-parents would really rather that the children had never been born.

Most of those professionally concerned with stepfamilies are practitioners first and scientists second. Fearing the insidious effects of 'self-fulfilling prophecies', they have understandably made it their business to offer cheerleaderly encouragement. Unfortunately, in attempting to counteract stepfamily 'myths', they have created a counter-factual mythology of their own, in which social relationships can be reordered by fiat and the statistical facts about differential violence can be dismissed. We doubt that this flight from reality is helpful, and not just because distortions like those in the AMA's report on 'Adolescents as victims of family violence' are more likely to impede child-protection efforts than to facilitate them. Stepfamilies are over-represented among the clients of marital counsellors, too, and their distress is unlikely to be alleviated by 'role theory'. Might it not be helpful if the step-parent's ambivalent and sometimes aggrieved feelings were acknowledged as normal, and if the genetic parent were encouraged to express appreciation for step-parental investment rather than to demand it as one's due? In fact, effective family therapists already have an intuitive understanding of this reality. A more principled understanding can only be to the good.

CHAPTER 7

··

Living in Step

Cautionary tales

In the Canadian and British homicide archives that we discussed in Chapter 4, there were dozens of children slain by stepfathers for every one killed by a stepmother. This imbalance is also conspicuous, if not quite so large, in the data archives of non-lethal child abuse. Does this mean that it is really only stepfatherhood that is a threat to children?

No, that is not the implication. Remember that stepmotherhood is itself rare, especially for the very youngest children. Indeed, stepmothers are so infrequent, both in the population-at-large and in the homicide and abuse data archives, that we have been reluctant to compute per capita rates and odds ratios, because the estimates are so sensitive to the effects of one or a few cases. Nevertheless, it is clear that stepmothers as well as stepfathers are greatly over-represented in child maltreatment, and our best estimate is that the hazards are roughly comparable. In the large data archives of the American Humane Association, the odds ratio by which homes with stepmothers exceed chance expectation is actually greater than the corresponding excess of homes with stepfathers, and the same is true of the families of origin of homeless adolescents in New York. In the Korean study, schoolchildren from the relatively few stepmother homes reported identical frequencies of being beaten as did those from stepfather homes, both substantially in excess of what was reported by children living with two genetic parents.

But if stepmotherhood is as risky as stepfatherhood — or even if it is riskier — the absolute quantity of violent and lethal abuse perpetrated by the more numerous stepfathers nonetheless exceeds that performed by their female counterparts. So why are wicked stepmothers so much more numerous in folklore than wicked stepfathers? A partial answer may be that stepmothers were not always so rare. Until this century, stepfamilies in Europe and America were more likely to be formed in the aftermath of a death than a divorce, and the mothers of young children incurred substantial mortality in childbirth and from other causes. Widowers often, though by no means always, kept the children and tried to import a replacement for their mother.

Another possible reason why Cinderella and Snow White were beset by stepmothers rather than stepfathers has to do with the social purposes of story-tellers. If a tale is to persist through the ages, it must appeal not only to its audience but also to its performers. So who were the story-tellers who found these tales to be worthy of the telling, and who were their listeners? If the primary audiences were small children, as they surely were for *Cinderella* and *Snow White*, the primary story-tellers were probably their mothers. And it is easy to imagine why mothers might prefer stories whose subtext is 'remember, my dears, that the worst thing imaginable would be for me to disappear and for your father to replace me' over those that instead whispered 'should your father ever die or leave us, it would be a terrible thing for you if I were to remarry'.

Step-parental investment in what?

By now, you may be thinking that the puzzle is not why step-relationships are difficult, but why they usually work out reasonably well. Why do they even exist?

The theories and evidence that we have reviewed can easily be read as implying that natural selection should have equipped any parentally investing creature with psychological defences against becoming an investing step-parent. Indeed, this was essentially the logic that motivated Harry Power's mountain-bluebird study, described near the outset of Chapter 3, and the results largely supported his prediction that replacement mates would not help rear their predecessors' young. However, this result is by no means universal. In fact, there was already quite a lot of evidence contrary to Power's prediction long before he ever conducted his research, as ornithologist Sievert Rohwer has pointed out.

If a peregrine falcon of either sex loses its mate while young are still dependent, a replacement mate is likely to appear quickly, and it will routinely behave in a fashion that looks just like the efforts of a genetic parent. Many other bird species do likewise. However, there are other birds that typically behave as Power reported, ignoring the young in the nest, and there are still others that kill them. What explains the differences? Rohwer suggested that the particular ecological and social circumstances of different species determine the costs and benefits of the alternatives and hence which evolves to be typical in any given case. In certain contexts – such as in populations in which parents routinely divorce and disperse after nesting failures (as many do), or when re-nesting within the same season is impossible anyway – infanticide will not help the killer re-nest sooner, and is therefore of little or no use; so ignoring or adopting young may then be favoured. Where selection appears to have favoured adopting one's predecessor's young as one's own is where breeding territories or mates are scarce, and are retained for a long time once they have been acquired. In these circumstances, step-parental investment is evidently the price paid for future breeding opportunities with the genetic parent. What has yet to be investigated is whether peregrines and other step-parenting birds still exhibit something less than a genetic parent's commitment, as they might be shown to do in a context such as defending the young against a predator who also represents a threat to the parent's own life.

Essentially the same argument has been invoked to explain observations of step-parental investment in other animals besides birds. In the tiny anemone fish, for example, suitable breeding sites are scarce and un-mated adults of both sexes are numerous, so if one member of a monogamous pair loses its mate, a new suitor finds step-parenting an acceptable courtship expense. Male baboons are sometimes solicitous towards particular infants that they could not possibly have sired, and this behaviour, too, has been interpreted as courtship effort, with the payoff coming in the form of an increased chance to sire the mother's next baby.

The human case seems to us analogous. Step-parents are primarily replacement mates, and only secondarily replacement parents. They assume their pseudo-parental obligations in the context of a web of reciprocities with the genetic parent, who is likely to recognize more or less explicitly that the new mate's tolerance and invest-ment constitute benefits bestowed on the genetic parent and the child, entitling the step-parent to reciprocal considerations. And once having opted in to this situ-ation, why shouldn't a reasonably well-appreciated step-parent be kindly, and even affectionate? After all, violent hostility is episodic and amicableness is frequent even among non-relatives. People thrive by the maintenance of networks of reciprocity and by establishing reputations that will make them attractive exchange partners, with the result that the desire to be generous and humane, and to be seen as generous and humane, is as human and as functional as more conflictual motives. There is thus no great conundrum in the fact that people treat their stepchildren for the most part quite tolerantly, nor even in their accepting some share of the costs of raising those children. But the fact of such investment cannot be taken to imply that step-parents will often come to feel the same sort of love and commitment as is ordinarily felt by genetic parents.

The profundity of parental love

The proposition that stepchildren are not loved like genetic children strikes many social scientists as distasteful. We believe that it is this distaste that has motivated the curious attempts, which we discussed in Chapter 6, to sweep the data away. Ironically, this dismissive stance tends to go hand in hand with an assumption that interpersonal attachments are arbitrary 'social constructions', an assumption that implicitly denies the profundity of parental love and can lead to such inhumane policy prescriptions as have sometimes arisen in extremist Utopian communities, in which infants were removed from their parents to be reared by child-care professionals.

Is the Darwinian world-view uglier in its implications? We think not. More generally, we reject the curiously prevalent notion that a scientific, materialistic, Darwinian world-view is uglier than its anti-scientific alternatives.

Instead, we would suggest that more realistic world-views invite more humane attitudes and practices than fantastic ones, because they entail better models of human nature and hence greater sensitivity to human needs and desires.

How to allocate one's efforts after 'remarriage' is a challenging problem that confronted hundreds of the ancestors of every person now living. No doubt indulgence towards a mate's children often had social uses. But it must rarely have been the case that a stepchild's welfare was as valuable to one's expected fitness as one's own child's welfare. A hypothetical psyche that treated stepchildren and genetic children exactly alike would be a psyche vulnerable to exploitation, and would be evolutionarily unstable in competition with more discriminating alternatives. There is, then, a strong theoretical rationale for expecting that the evolved human psyche contains safeguards against allowing a mere stepchild, however appealing, easy access to that special mental category occupied by genetic children, the appropriate objects for the most nearly selfless love we know.

To the best of our knowledge, the research findings about stepfamily life are fully consistent with this Darwinian analysis.

SUGGESTIONS FOR FURTHER READING

Booth, Alan and Judy Dunn (eds.), *Stepfamilies: Who Benefits? Who Does Not?*, Hillsdale, NJ: Lawrence Erlbaum (1994).

Cox, Marian Emily Roalfe, *Cinderella: Three Hundred and Forty-five Variants of Cinderella, Catskin, and Cap o' Rushes, abstracted and tabulated with a discussion of mediaeval analogues, and notes*, London: The Folklore Society (1893).

Cronin, Helena, *The Ant and the Peacock*, Cambridge: Cambridge University Press (1992).

Daly, Martin and Margo Wilson, *Homicide*, New York: Aldine de Gruyter (1988).

Daly, Martin and Margo Wilson, 'Discriminative parental solicitude and the relevance of evolutionary models to the analysis of motivational systems', in M.S. Gazzaniga (ed.), *The Cognitive Neurosciences*, Cambridge, MA: MIT Press (1995).

Dundes, Alan, *Cinderella: A Casebook*, New York: Wildman Press (1983).

Ferri, Elsa, *Stepchildren: A National study*, Windsor: NFER-Nelson (1984).

Gelles, Richard J. and Jane B. Lancaster (eds.), *Child Abuse and Neglect: Biosocial Dimensions*, New York: Aldine de Gruyter (1987).

Hausfater, Glenn and Sarah Blaffer Hrdy (eds.), *Infanticide*, New York: Aldine de Gruyter (1984).

Parmigiani, Stefano and Frederick S. vom Saal (eds.), *Infanticide and Parental Care*, Chur, Switzerland: Harwood Academic (1994).

Rohwer, Sievert, 'Selection for adoption versus infanticide by replacement "mates" in birds', *Current Ornithology* 3, 353–395 (1986).

Trivers, Robert L., *Social Evolution*, Menlo Park, CA: Benjamin/Cummings (1985).

Williams, George C., *Adaptation and Natural Selection*, Princeton, NJ: Princteon University Press (1966).